DEPRESSION-ERA MURALS OF THE BAY AREA

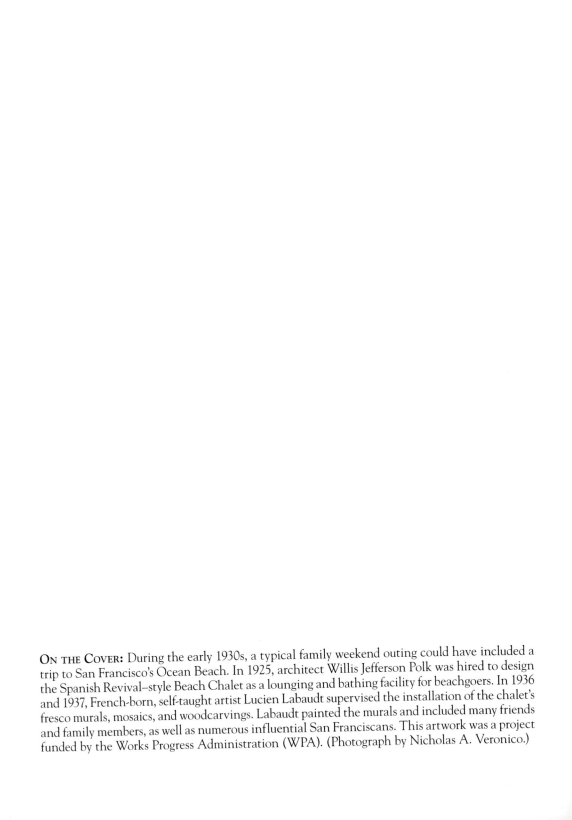

DEPRESSION-ERA MURALS OF THE BAY AREA

Nicholas A. Veronico, Gina F. Morello,
Brett A. Casadonte, and Gilda Collins

ARCADIA
PUBLISHING

Published by Arcadia Publishing
Charleston, South Carolina

Printed in the United States of America

Library of Congress Control Number: 2013949236

For all general information, please contact Arcadia Publishing:
Telephone 843-853-2070
Fax 843-853-0044
E-mail sales@arcadiapublishing.com
For customer service and orders:
Toll-Free 1-888-313-2665

Visit us on the Internet at www.arcadiapublishing.com

For the artist Ray Bingham (aka L. Ray)
For Nell and Joseph Morello
For the Casadontes—Arthur and Janice,
Dominic, Maximilian, and Alexandra
For Timothy and Edith Collins

CONTENTS

FOREWORD

The incredible legacy of New Deal art can be seen today on public buildings, but thousands of artworks have been languishing unseen in museum vaults since the 1940s. Hopefully, a future national New Deal museum could interpret, on a permanent basis, not only the art but also the architecture and social programs of the New Deal. Until that time, other resources are needed either online or in book form. *Depression-Era Murals of the Bay Area* provides an essential guide to key public artworks in the Bay Area.

The government's response to the Great Depression was unprecedented—an all-out investment in getting America back on its feet. Within a decade, it provided a multitude of jobs and social programs. Extensive environmental restoration revitalized forests and depleted farmland. The government launched vast projects nationwide to provide clean water, waste treatment, and electricity. The legacy of the New Deal includes thousands of schools, museums, parks, hospitals, roads, airports, post offices, and public buildings, and much of this public space is adorned by the works of artists and craftspeople. The scenes and themes portrayed in these decades-old works still inspire viewers; some are still relevant to today's social and economic conditions.

The massive federal efforts to improve employment, housing, education, health care, arts, agriculture, civil works, conservation, banking, and labor have been largely forgotten. Social programs such as unemployment and retirement insurance, daycare programs, and student lunch programs also helped families come out of poverty. Myriad educational and job training programs led millions of Americans to higher standards of living, and worker safety, public health, and cultural programs elevated Americans' quality of life.

Unprecedented government support allowed a flowering of grassroots innovation and creativity. This volume will not only encourage exploration and viewing of some New Deal–era signature accomplishments, it will serve to rekindle pride in this extraordinary period of American history.

Harvey Smith
President, National New Deal Preservation Association
Project Advisor, the Living New Deal

ACKNOWLEDGEMENTS

Depression-Era Murals of the Bay Area is a celebration of one of this nation's most prolific periods in public art. At the time, many of the artisans were in dire financial straits, much like their neighbors. The Great Depression impacted everyone. That said, the legacy of such hard times is now visible in a body of work created by some of the most talented and visionary artists in the nation.

More than 80 years after the peak of the Great Depression, a cadre of talented and knowledgeable people now serve as stewards of the many murals shown within these pages; it is their generosity that brings *Depression-Era Murals of the Bay Area* to life.

The authors wish to express their appreciation and thanks to the following: Gina Bardi at the San Francisco Maritime Museum Library (National Park Service); Julia Bergman and William Maynez, custodians of the Diego Rivera Pan American Unity mural and others at the City College of San Francisco; Erin Garcia and Sue Grinols at the Fine Arts Museums of San Francisco; Dana Ketcham, Jim Jackson, and Marcus Santiago at the San Francisco Recreation and Parks Department; Jared Nelson and Sara Miller at Arcadia Publishing; Anne Marie Purkey Levine and Kate Patterson of the San Francisco Arts Commission; Hannah Rhadigan of the Artists Rights Society; Anne Rosenthal of Anne Rosenthal Fine Art; Harvey Smith of the National New Deal Preservation Association; M. Lee Stone of M. Lee Stone Fine Prints, Inc.; Peter Summerville of the Treasure Island Development Authority; Coma Te, Ericka Lovrin, and Eric Guthertz of the San Francisco Unified School District; Jeff Thomas at the San Francisco Public Library; Abbie Tuller and Joe Fitting at the San Francisco Zoo; Betty S. Veronico; and Amanda Williford of the National Park Service.

Unless otherwise noted, all images appear courtesy of the authors.

With sincere appreciation,

Nicholas A. Veronico
Gina F. Morello
Brett Casadonte
Gilda Collins

INTRODUCTION

Each year, millions of guests visit Bay Area locations lined with Depression-era murals, from the Lillian Coit Memorial Tower (Coit Tower) to many of the area's post offices. Do those visitors realize what they are looking at, who the artists were, or what the art depicts and represents?

These beautiful murals were born in a time gripped by a worldwide economic depression. In the United States, many identify the start of the Great Depression with the stock market crash of October 29, 1929. In the ensuing years, credit dried up, and those with money were not buying big-ticket items, which resulted in a lack of sales that translated into layoffs in the manufacturing sector. A severe drought that strangled agricultural production in the Midwestern United States compounded the problem, leading to the failure of thousands of family farms and putting more people out of work. In 1933, unemployment in the United States reached nearly 25 percent.

In an attempt to protect their economies, the United States and other nations began enacting tariffs on imports, virtually halting global trade. One problem worsened the next—the crash of the stock market and resulting loss of personal wealth dramatically impacted consumer confidence, which led to the lack of sales that reduced demand for goods and caused layoffs, and without income or the prospect of work, many became homeless.

The creative trades were hit hardest in the depressed economy, especially professional artists and sculptors. Pres. Franklin D. Roosevelt was inaugurated on March 4, 1933, and the problems he faced were enormous. His election platform promised a "New Deal" for Americans, and his economic and financial reform programs and policies came under this heading.

On May 9, 1933, lawyer-turned-artist George Biddle, a student of Mexican artist Diego Rivera, wrote to fellow Harvard University and Groton School alumnus Roosevelt about the plight of artists and suggested a federal program to support the arts. Biddle's correspondence and relationship with the president is widely credited with prompting Roosevelt's efforts to provide relief to artists through the formation of the Advisory Committee to the Treasury on Fine Arts.

Based upon recommendations from the Advisory Committee to the Treasury on Fine Arts, the first of four New Deal art programs, the Public Works of Art Project (PWAP), was created on December 8, 1933. PWAP only lasted for one year—from 1933 to 1934. The project put artists on the government payroll and gave them a weekly paycheck. By the end of its one-year operation, PWAP employed nearly 14,000 artists who, in total, created more than 15,000 works of art.

During the ensuing decade, three other artist-relief projects were created under the New Deal: the Treasury Department's Section of Painting and Sculpture, the Treasury Relief Art Project, and the Federal Art Project.

The Treasury Department initiated the Section of Painting and Sculpture in 1934 to replace the PWAP. In 1939, the Section of Painting and Sculpture was redefined as the Section of Fine Arts and is more commonly referred to as "the Section." This program offered commissions to artists and sculptors through a competitive bid process and paid a lump sum for artwork, often tens of times more than the weekly wage paid to those working in relief roles. In 1940, for example, 82 artists submitted designs to the Section's jury, who awarded Anton Refregier the commission to fill the Rincon Annex Post Office with murals. Refregier's commission was $26,000—at the time, a modest home cost $3,900. When the Section of Fine Arts program was terminated in 1942, it had commissioned more than 1,300 murals and 300 sculptures.

The Treasury Relief Art Project (TRAP) lasted from 1935 to 1938 and sought to create art for federal government buildings. TRAP drew its creative cadre from relief rolls and employed more than 400 artists. TRAP was unique in that its artwork was specifically loaned to agencies of the federal government.

In April 1937, many WPA workers went on strike for a 10-percent increase in pay. While on strike, they were not paid, thereby inadvertently helping the WPA reduce costs. These picketers are striking outside of the recreational projects office at Seventh and Bryant Streets. They were joined by many WPA artists. (San Francisco Public Library.)

The Works Progress Administration's Federal Art Project (FAP), which existed from 1935 to 1942, was the largest of the government's art initiatives. According to the final report on the WPA Program, from 1935 to 1943, FAP "produced over 108,000 easel paintings, 11,300 fine prints, 2,500 murals, and 18,000 sculpture works." Artists on the FAP payroll were paid, on average, $24 per week.

It is important to note that PWAP, the Section, and TRAP programs were overseen by the US Treasury Department, while FAP was administered by the WPA. Under the 1939 Reorganization Act, all four programs were consolidated into the newly formed Federal Works Agency.

In addition to the federal artist relief programs, California received federal funds administered at the state level by the State Emergency Relief Administration (SERA). This agency was subsequently replaced by the California State Relief Administration (SRA) in 1935.

Bay Area artists also benefitted from the Golden Gate International Exposition (GGIE), held east of San Francisco on Treasure Island, which is located at the midpoint of the San Francisco-Oakland Bay Bridge. The GGIE ran from February 18, 1939, to October 29, 1939, and again from May 25, 1940, to September 29, 1940.

One of the featured attractions was Art in Action, organized by the GGIE committee that included architect Timothy Pflueger. The exhibition featured live demonstrations by artists such as Diego Rivera and sculptor Dudley C. Carter, and much of the finished art was bound for display at the Ocean Campus of the San Francisco Junior College (now the City College of San Francisco), where Pflueger was the architect of the science building.

In the late 1920s and early 1930s, a number of Bay Area artists who would later prominently feature in the region's many Depression-era art projects studied under painter Diego Rivera at his Mexico City studio. Rivera's students included Maxine Albro, Victor Arnautoff, Ray Boynton,

Ralph Stackpole, Clifford Wight, and Bernard Zakheim. Rivera came to the United States in 1930 to paint a mural, known as *Allegory of California*, in the stock exchange on Stockton Street and subsequently painted *The Making of a Fresco Showing the Building of a City* at the California School of Fine Arts (now the San Francisco Art Institute) at 800 Chestnut Street.

For the GGIE, Rivera undertook a project that involved painting an 1,800-square-foot (22 feet tall by 74 feet wide) fresco mural, which he titled *The Marriage of the Artistic Expression of the North and of the South on this Continent*, although it is commonly referred to as the Pan American Unity mural.

During Art in Action, the public could watch assistants grinding pigments for the Rivera mural; sculptors, weavers, and jewelers at work; potters spinning clay blocks into functional wares; artists making prints from linoleum blocks; and mosaic artisans creating colorful tile works. For many spectators, it was their first exposure to "artists in action."

Miguel Covarrubias, a Mexican artist known in the United States for his illustrations in *Vanity Fair* and *The New Yorker*, created six mural maps of the Pacific region, each with a different theme; they were collectively known as the *Pageant of the Pacific*. The murals were displayed in the GGIE's Pacific House and included *Peoples, Art and Culture, Economy, Native Dwellings, Native Means of Transportation*, and *The Fauna and Flora of the Pacific* (the largest mural, measuring 15 feet tall by 24 feet wide), which is now on display at the de Young Museum in Golden Gate Park.

SAN FRANCISCO ARTISTS' AND WRITERS' UNION

In the fall of 1933, poet Kenneth Rexroth and painter Bernard Zakheim were instrumental in establishing the San Francisco Artists' and Writers' Union. By 1934, the group had more than 350 members, although it was not technically a "union" but more of a social/political action and networking organization for creative types during tumultuous times.

In 1932, the Rockefeller family commissioned Diego Rivera to paint a mural in the nearly completed Rockefeller Center. Rivera's resulting fresco, *Man at the Crossroads*, featured an image of Communist leader Vladimir Lenin; this upset the Rockefellers, and in May 1933, they paid Rivera and had him escorted from the building before covering the unfinished mural with canvas. In February 1934, the mural was covertly destroyed overnight. Artists across the nation decried this act of censorship, including those in the Bay Area with strong ties to Rivera. On February 14, 1934, Maxine Albro read the union's manifesto on the destruction of Rivera's mural on the steps of Coit Tower.

Soon after the removal of Rivera's mural, the International Longshoremen's Association (ILA) and other unions struck ports up and down the West Coast in May 1934. Clashes with police and National Guardsmen resulted in dozens wounded and four killed. As the strike raged along the waterfront at the base of Telegraph Hill, many claimed the labor unrest was influenced by members of the communist party.

Simultaneously, the PWAP took notice of blatant communist references in the Coit Tower murals painted by Victor Arnautoff, John Langley Howard, Clifford Wight, and Bernard Zakheim. Wight's mural contained a length of cable with the hammer-and-sickle insignia surrounded by the words "workers of the world unite." Coit Tower was closed to the public as controversy raged about the murals. Eventually, the PWAP allowed Arnautoff's, Howard's, and Zakheim's subtle references but insisted on removing Wight's hammer and sickle. Coit Tower reopened to the public, and artists across the nation realized that anti-American references would not be tolerated in public art.

In addition to numerous public art projects in the Bay Area, artists were able to secure mural commissions in a variety of commercial buildings. In 1932, at the height of the Depression, Arnautoff was commissioned to paint four frescoes at the new Palo Alto Medical Clinic. The breasts of a young woman undergoing an exam in one of the panels were fodder for scandal at the time.

In this picture taken on February 14, 1934, on the steps of Coit Tower on San Francisco's Telegraph Hill, Maxine Albro (center, in white coveralls) reads the San Francisco Artists' and Writers' Union's manifesto on the destruction of Diego Rivera's mural in New York's Rockefeller Center. Pictured here are muralist and project coordinator Victor Arnautoff (third from left, facing the camera), Ray Boynton (fifth from left), Helen Clement Mills (10th from left), George Harris (11th from left), Bernard Zakheim (sixth from right), and Julia H. Rogers (fifth from right, in coveralls). (San Francisco Public Library.)

THE DEPRESSION ERA COMES TO A CLOSE

America's entry into World War II immediately following the December 7, 1941, attack on Pearl Harbor essentially marked the end of the Great Depression, and the nation transitioned to a wartime economy. The days of unemployment for individuals faded into the past just as the days of underemployment for most industries began as the majority of able-bodied men were shipped off to fight in the war.

Four months after the Pearl Harbor attack, most of the WPA and FAP projects were brought to a halt on April 18, 1942, the same day Lt. Col. Jimmy Doolittle led 16 B-25 bombers off the deck of the aircraft carrier USS *Hornet* in an attack on Japan's main islands. On June 30, 1943, as the tide of World War II was shifting in favor of the Allies, the WPA was terminated and ceased to exist. Some WPA/FAP artists joined the military, plying their trade for the armed services or creating posters for the home front war effort. Some WPA commissions that were already funded took until 1946 to be completed; however, times had changed, and the era of Depression-subsidized art had passed into history.

MURAL TYPES AND STYLES

Depression-era murals in the Bay Area were typically created using one of three distinct techniques: Fresco (*buon fresco*), Egg Tempera (*fresco secco*), and Oil on canvas (*marouflage*). All three types of murals can be found in some locations, such as Coit Tower.

Fresco

Water-based paint is applied to wet lime plaster, and the paint dries to become an integral part of the plaster. To begin, a base layer of plaster is laid down; once it is dry, the artist draws his or her design. Once the guide drawing is completed, a second, thin layer of plaster is applied—enough for one day's work, since the artist can only paint as long as the plaster is wet. Each day, the process is repeated until the mural is complete.

Egg Tempera

Pure egg yolk (no whites) is combined with ground, dry pigments and water to form paint. Whites make the paint dry faster, so care is taken to completely separate the yolks. The paint is applied to the drying plaster, with the egg yolk serving as a binding agent between the pigment and the plaster. Egg tempera is applied to plaster that is "tacky" as opposed to the wet plaster used in fresco painting.

Oil on Canvas

Pigments are combined with an oil medium, such as linseed oil, to form paint. The paint is then applied directly onto wooden panels or to a canvas stretched over a wooden frame. Some people hold the opinion that this style of mural is preferable, as it can be removed from a wall and transported and is not susceptible to cracking under environmental stress, such as during an earthquake.

Many of the Depression-era murals survive today thanks to caretakers who recognized the need to have the artwork restored by professional conservators. The Bay Area is home to a number of professionals; one is Anne Rosenthal, who used her talents to conserve Hilaire Hiler's Atlantis and Mu mural at the Aquatic Park Bathhouse at the foot of Polk Street. The National Park Service recently reopened the Aquatic Park Bathhouse Building (Maritime Museum) after a multiyear restoration of the building and its artwork. (Anne Rosenthal.)

Artist Edith Hamlin's 9-foot-by-12-foot fresco *Hunting in California* depicts scenes of duck hunting in the San Francisco Bay Delta region. The vibrant colors of the hunter, his ducks, and the golden-hued background are as bright today as they were when painted 80 years ago. Hamlin's fresco surrounds the second-floor elevator door in Coit Tower. (Photograph by Brett Casadonte.)

One

THE IMPRESSIVE COIT TOWER

The Lillian Coit Memorial Tower sits on Telegraph Hill, offering 360-degree views of the waterfront and bay. Telegraph Hill—so named during the Gold Rush of 1849—was a place where signalers could communicate with ships entering the harbor through the use of flag semaphore.

The tower's namesake, Lillian "Lillie" (Hitchcock) Colt, was born in Maryland in 1844 and came to San Francisco at age seven, when her father, an Army doctor, was transferred to the Presidio. In the late 1850s, as a teenager, she helped rally men to come to the aid of the volunteer fire department's Knickerbocker Engine Company No. 5, which saved a structure on Telegraph Hill. She subsequently became an honorary member of Knickerbocker Engine Company No. 5.

In 1863, Lillie married Howard Coit, a wealthy investor; Howard passed away in 1885. Upon her death in July 1929, Lillie left one-third of her estate to the City and County of San Francisco for the "purpose of adding to the beauty of the city." The city took Coit's $118,000 bequest, added $7,000 to round the number up to $125,000, and awarded architect Arthur Brown Jr. the commission to build a memorial. He designed a cast concrete, 180-foot-tall tower atop a 32-foot-tall base.

In December 1933, with the tower complete but devoid of decoration on the inside, the Public Works of Art Project (PWAP) sought to fill the first- and second-floor walls with frescoes. Victor Arnautoff was selected to paint a mural and to serve as a foreman overseeing the other artists.

A total of 26 artists and 19 assistants painted 27 murals (3,691 square feet of murals), 20 of which are open to the public on the first floor, inside Coit Tower. The tower contains the following frescoes: Maxine Albro's (1903–1966) *California*; Victor Arnautoff's (1896–1979) *City Life*; Ray Bertrand's (1909–1986) *Meat Industry*; Ray Boynton's (1883–1951) *Animal Force* and *Machine Force*; Mallette Harold Dean's (1907–1975) *Stockbroker* and *Scientist-Inventor*; George Harris's (1913–1991) *Banking and Law*; William Hesthal's (1908–1985) *Railroad and Shipping*; John Langley Howard's (1902–1999) *California Industrial Scenes*; Gordon Langdon's (1910–1963) *California Agricultural Industry*; Frederick Olmsted's (1911–1990) *Power*; Suzanne Scheuer's (1898–1984) *Newsgathering*; Ralph Stackpole's (1885–1973) *Industries of California*; Frede Vidar's (1911–1967) *Department Store*; Clifford Wight's (1900–1966) *Surveyor, Ironworker, Cowboy*, and *Farmer*; and Bernard Zakheim's (1896–1985) *Library*.

The first floor also contains five oil-on-canvas murals, titled *Bay Area Hills*, by Rinaldo Cuneo (1877–1939); Jose Moya Del Pino's (1891–1969) *San Francisco Bay, North*; and three by Otis Oldfield (1890–1969)—*San Francisco Bay, Seabirds*, and *Bay Area Map*.

There are five fresco murals in the stairwell leading up to and on the second floor, including Jane Berlandina's (1898–1970) *Home Life*; Parker Hall's (1898–1982) *Collegiate Sports*; Edith Hamlin's (1902–1992) *Hunting in California*; Lucien Labaudt's (1880–1943) *Powell Street*; and Edward Terada's (1908–1993) *Sports*. The stairwell and second-floor murals are only accessible during the tower's Saturday guided tours; visit www.sfrecpark.org for more information.

If one image in the Coit Tower illustrates the depths of despair of the Great Depression, it is John Langley Howard's *California Industrial Scenes*. This panel shows men of all ages and races wearing despondent looks as they face zero prospects of work. Another part of the mural shows the contrast of a homeless family camping near their broken-down Model T Ford as a group of wealthy people looks on while standing in front of a limousine. (Photograph by Nicholas A. Veronico.)

Artist William Hesthal's *Railroad and Shipping* presents a view of commerce in action—trains moving freight and ships loaded with cargo. The transport of goods provides jobs, which in turn creates demand. The engine is Southern Pacific No. 2432 (Pacific Class P-3), set up with four leading, six driving, and two trailing wheels (4-6-2). The engine, built by the Baldwin Locomotive Works, typically ran between Sacramento and Oakland. (Photograph by Nicholas A. Veronico.)

Animal Force and Machine Force is Ray Boynton's interpretation of how America's economy was changing from an agrarian society, in which productivity was measured by how much a person could produce with the assistance of an animal, to an industrial society, in which machines could greatly multiply a person's productivity. (Photograph by Nicholas A. Veronico.)

This photograph shows Boynton painting the farm scene inside the tower's main entrance. (San Francisco Public Library.)

Victor Arnautoff (standing) and his assistant Tom Hayes fill in the *City Life* mural on the south side of the Coit Tower's interior. Arnautoff is painting the hat of a man being robbed at gunpoint. To the right of the man, the headline of the topmost newspaper in the rack reads, "Police Robbed, Accuse Dillinger." In the background, people go about their daily lives in the city as rescue workers tend to a traffic accident. (Right, San Francisco Public Library; below, photograph by Nicholas A. Veronico.)

The left panel of Victor Arnautoff's *City Life* is a series of vignettes that capture San Francisco, from its industrial heart to one of the statues created by Ralph Stackpole (also a Coit Tower artist) in front of the Pacific Stock Exchange building to the hustle and bustle of commuters traveling to work. Many of the Coit Tower artists lived or had studios at the intersection of Washington and Montgomery Streets, hence the sign in the center foreground. The fire truck coming down

the hill to aid the accident victims bears the number "5" in tribute to Lillie Hitchcock Coit's fascination with the local Knickerbocker Engine Company No. 5. Note the natural-gas tank (in the upper left background) that was once located along the waterfront and the architecture of the gas station (center) with pumps that had glass globes on top to advertise different brands of gasoline. (Photograph by Brett Casadonte.)

City Life is 10 feet tall and 36 feet wide. Artist Victor Arnautoff included a self-portrait on the right side of the mural; he stands next to a newspaper rack filled with publications promoting Communist ideologies—eStampa, Daily Worker, and the New Masses, an illustrated magazine that included contributors such as Jack London, Carl Sandburg, and Louise Bryant. (Photograph by Nicholas A. Veronico.)

Maxine Albro's California is notable for its extensive use of vibrant red, yellow, and orange hues. California is 10 feet tall and 42 feet wide and faces the east windows of the Coit Tower lobby. Albro studied with Diego Rivera's assistant Paul O'Higgins in Mexico and had the opportunity to watch Rivera paint frescoes firsthand. (Photograph by Nicholas A. Veronico.)

Compare the image at right—of Lucien Labaudt painting one of the two 6-by-32-foot panels of *Powell Street*, located in the Coit Tower's stairwell—with the finished mural (below). The "Wed." under Labaudt's brush is the abbreviation for Wednesday, and the pencil delineates the border of where he planned to work that day. His original intention was to include another well-dressed woman walking behind the iceman and ahead of the mailman, but that appeared to block too much of the cable car, so he replaced her with the boy on a skateboard-type scooter. Note that the mailman's satchel is closed in the pencil drawing but brimming with packages in the final mural. (Right, San Francisco Public Library; below, photograph by Brett Casadonte.)

Ralph Stackpole's *Industries of California* is adjacent to Ray Boynton's *Animal Force and Machine Force* mural in the tower's lobby. The transition between the two is dramatic. *Industries of California* depicts workers as subservient to the giant machinery that drives manufacturing in the Golden State, from oil refineries and chemical plants to the state's nearly extinct steel industry to the labor-intensive canning and packing plants. (Photograph by Brett Casadonte.)

The right side of artist George Harris's 10-foot-by-10-foot *Banking and Law* fresco shows writers updating commodity trading numbers next to a stock chart showing a massive decline. At lower right in the image, armed guards protect bagged coins and currency, while the attorneys on the left pore through books in a law library. The titles of the books list many of his fellow artists as authors; some of the titles are considered derogatory. (Photograph by Brett Casadonte.)

The right-side detail of Bernard Zakheim's *Library* fresco depicts men reading in the periodical room. Most of the "readers" are friends and fellow artists, while the headlines provide social commentary on the times. For example, Ralph Stackpole's newspaper bears the headline "Local Artists Protest Destruction of Rivera's Fresco," while Beniamino Bufano holds a paper proclaiming "B. Bufano's St. Francis Just Around the Corner: Art Commission Awakens from It's [*sic*] Deep Sleep." Zakheim's inclusion of the book *Das Kapital*, by Karl Marx, and painting of the names of many prominent Communists—such as writer and activist Maxim Gorky and American Marxist Granville Hicks—on the spines of books stoked the uproar over Communist symbols in the Coit Tower murals. (Photograph by Nicholas A. Veronico.)

Ralph Chessé painted a park scene called *Children at Play*, which occupies a nine-by-six-foot wall on the tower's second floor. In the center of the mural is this boy holding a toy airplane and dressed as Charles A. Lindbergh, who had crossed the Atlantic Ocean six years before planning began for the mural. "Lucky Lindy" was still prominent in the news, and many young people wanted to be just like him. (Photograph by Nicholas A. Veronico.)

Japanese-born artist Edward Takeo Terada painted a fresco on two adjoining walls on the tower's second floor. The panel on the east wall, *Sports*, depicts golfers and hurdlers, while the south wall panel (above) is filled with four polo players in action. The second floor of the Coit Tower contains an anteroom outside the area that once housed the caretaker's quarters. The room's 306 square feet of wall space holds Jane Berlandina's egg tempera *Home Life* frescoes, one of which is pictured below, in which families are playing cards, working in the kitchen, and entertaining in the parlor while dancing and playing a variety of musical instruments. Berlandina limited the color palate to reds, browns, and yellows and used thin white lines to outline parts of the mural. The sharp contrast between *Home Life* and the more colorful murals in the tower's lobby have given rise to the impression that Berlandina's frescoes are unfinished. Upon closer inspection, they are highly detailed and very unique. (Both photographs by Nicholas A. Veronico.)

Collegiate Sports adorns two walls at the top of the staircase leading from the first to the second floor. Painted by artist Parker Hall, who was married to Maxine Albro, the panels depict athletic opportunities available to students who continue their education past high school. This football player dominates the archway above the door. (Photograph by Nicholas A. Veronico.)

This is a detail from Rinaldo Cuneo's *Bay Area Hills*, a pair of oil-on-canvas murals depicting agricultural life in San Francisco's East Bay. This farmer plowing the field on a tractor is the central figure in one of the panels located in the tower's elevator lobby. (Photograph by Nicholas A. Veronico.)

This photograph of the downstairs lobby of the Beach Chalet shows one panel of Lucien Labaudt's nine-foot-tall *San Francisco Life* fresco. The building sits at the western edge of Golden Gate Park and faces San Francisco's famed Ocean Beach. *San Francisco Life* covers more than 1,500 square feet of wall space and depicts many different elements of life in the city. Within the fresco, Labaudt painted a self-portrait and included his family, a number of coworkers, and many important San Franciscans. (Photograph by Nicholas A. Veronico.)

Two

BEACH CHALET

The City of San Francisco built the Beach Chalet in 1925 for $60,000. Architect Willis J. Polk designed the building in the Spanish Revival style. The ground floor consisted of a lounge and changing rooms, which no longer exist; the second story held a 200-seat bar and restaurant that still operates today.

In 1936, under the auspices of the Works Progress Administration's Federal Art Project (FAP), French-born and self-taught artist Lucien Labaudt (1880–1943) was hired to adorn the first floor of the Beach Chalet with frescoes, mosaics, and woodcarvings. The frescoes are nine feet tall and cover more than 1,500 feet of wall space. Labaudt's assistants for the project were Arnold Bray and Farrell Dwyer, with James Wyatt preparing the plaster for the frescoes. The murals, titled *San Francisco Life*, consist of panels depicting scenes of Golden Gate Park, Fisherman's Wharf, and Land's End, among others. Labaudt liked to incorporate people from his life into his art, and he included his self-portrait in the Baker Beach scene.

Labaudt's murals depict a serene and simple San Francisco, in sharp contrast with the harsh reality of what many were experiencing during the Great Depression. The tile mosaics were also designed by Labaudt and were installed by Primo Caredio. Sculptor Michael von Meyer contributed an ornamental staircase balustrade made of magnolia wood and titled *Sea Creatures*. The Beach Chalet project was completed in 1939.

During the next 70-plus years, the Beach Chalet had many additional uses. In World War II, the army used it as the Coastal Defense Headquarters; in 1947, the Veterans of Foreign Wars occupied the second floor as meeting space while leasing the first floor out as a bar; the VFW left the building in 1979. In 1981, the National Park Service listed Beach Chalet in the National Register of Historic Places (number 179), but it remained closed until 1987, when the city allocated $800,000 for infrastructure repairs, including restoration of the WPA/FAP artwork. This work was completed in 1989, but the building remained closed until 1996, when the Friends of Recreation and Parks awarded a $1.5 million grant to the architecture firm Heller Manus to bring the building up to code. The Beach Chalet reopened its doors to the public in 1997.

The historic Beach Chalet is currently home to the Golden Gate Park Visitor's Center and features the amazing and historic WPA frescoes, mosaics, and woodcarvings created by Lucien Labaudt and his assistants. The chalet offers two eating establishments: the Park Chalet Garden Restaurant and the Beach Chalet Brewery and Restaurant. (Photograph by Nicholas A. Veronico.)

The north wall leading into the gift shop contains a mosaic work—designed by Labaudt and created by artist Primo R. Caredio—that depicts California poppies. Above the arch, Labaudt included a quote by American poet George Sterling: "At the end of our streets—the stars." (Photograph by Nicholas A. Veronico.)

This waterfront scene in front of San Francisco's Pier 26 includes a portrait of Lucien Labaudt's friend, Harry Bridges, pushing a hand truck. Bridges founded the International Longshoremen's and Warehousemen's Union (ILWU) Local 19 in 1937 and served as president of the organization for 40 years. (Photograph by Nicholas A. Veronico.)

This scene shows San Francisco's Fisherman's Wharf during the early 1930s. A women and a young girl watch a fisherman prepare a local Dungeness crab from the pots behind him. The man mending a fishing net in the background at far right is artist Primo R. Caredio, who created Beach Chalet's tiled mosaic. (Photograph by Nicholas A. Veronico.)

A family of beach enthusiasts heads to Baker Beach with fishing poles, straw mats, and blankets. Labaudt's nephew, Bill Chamberlain, and his fox terrier lead the way. The Land's End lookout building and the Marin Headlands are visible in the background. (Photograph by Nicholas A. Veronico.)

Golden Gate Park is shown in the background of this fresco that includes Beatrice Judd Ryan (WPA director of exhibitions), who is watching a WPA photographer take a picture of a girl on skates. Fresco assistant Arnold Bray (fourth from left) and artist Ben Cunningham (fifth from left) are also included. Spencer Mackey (School of Fine Arts director) is holding the leash of a Saint Bernard; this dog and his owner used to stop by the Beach Chalet every day while the frescoes were being painted, so Labaudt added the dog to the mural. Labaudt painted a dedication plaque in the lower left corner that includes the names of all who worked on the Beach Chalet project. (Photograph by Nicholas A. Veronico.)

This panel of the Baker Beach picnic scene shows many of Labaudt's family and friends. Sculptor Robert Howard is playing a harmonica, Labaudt's daughter Yliane is playing a guitar, and the sheet music, held by a man in a black suit (possibly mosaic tile artist Primo R. Caredio), is titled *Red River Valley*, arranged by Nick Mandloff. Labaudt's fresco assistants, Arnold Bray and Farrell Dwyer, are shown assisting his older daughter, Alvyne, who is cutting watermelon. Labaudt's wife, Marcelle, is reaching out to receive a bowl of potato salad. Mile Rock Lighthouse is visible at upper right behind the beachgoers. (Photograph by Nicholas A. Veronico.)

The center section of the Golden Gate Park fresco shows Phil Sears (WPA office worker) and Dorothy Collins (California Arts administrator) peering at a gray squirrel over the back of a park bench with artist William Gaskin (director of the San Francisco WPA) standing behind them. Joseph Danysh (then director of the California Federal Art Project) rides the white horse, and sculptor Beniamino Bufano is on the grey horse. Sitting on the other side of Collins on the park bench is John McLaren (Golden Gate Park superintendent for more than 50 years), who is being presented with a redwood sapling for his 90th birthday by Jack Spring (who later worked as the general manager of the San Francisco Recreation and Parks Department), who is holding the redwood's root ball. (Photograph by Nicholas A. Veronico.)

On the right side of the Golden Gate Park mural, four people are dressed in sporting outfits—Los Angeles artist Lorser Feitelson and his wife, Helen Lundeberg, are in tennis whites—along with two golf enthusiasts dressed in period outfits. Golden Gate Park's Japanese Tea House is visible in the background. (Photograph by Nicholas A. Veronico.)

In this panel, Labaudt painted three stylish women looking out to Land's End; from left to right are Beatrice Judd Ryan (WPA director of exhibitions), Marcelle Labaudt, and Dorothy Collins (California Arts administrator). Next to the women, a man with a 1930s motorcycle is admiring the scenic view. In the background, looking toward the Presidio, are the Legion of Honor Museum, the Veterans Administration Hospital, and a water tower at Fort Miley. (Photograph by Nicholas A. Veronico.)

As part of the Golden Gate Bridge's opening celebration, Gottardo Piazzoni hosted a grand Spanish celebration for which children dressed up as cowboys with holstered guns. The Marina district, in the background, shows motorboats and sailors in front of the St. Francis Yacht Club. (Photograph by Nicholas A. Veronico.)

Labaudt included a portrait of Arthur Brown Jr., co-architect of San Francisco's City Hall (which Brown designed in 1912 with partner John Bakewell), holding design plans for the Coit Tower, which he and Henry Howard developed. Inside Coit Tower, which was completed on October 8, 1933, Labaudt painted the Powell Street mural in the staircase leading from the first floor to the second floor. (Photograph by Nicholas A. Veronico.)

The arch on the south wall leads upstairs to the Beach Chalet Brewery and Restaurant. Above the arch, Labaudt included a quote by poet Joaquin Miller: "Sails are furl'd— From farthest corners of the world." To the right of the staircase, Labaudt's friend Gottardo Piazzoni is pictured talking to two young girls. Piazzoni was a Swiss-born landscape painter, muralist, and sculptor of Italian heritage; he was a key member of the school of Northern California artists in the early 1900s. (Photograph by Nicholas A. Veronico.)

Labaudt showed his humorous side when he chose this warrior launching an arrow as a guide for guests looking for the men's and women's restrooms. (Photograph by Nicholas A. Veronico.)

Michael von Meyer's staircase carvings, titled *Sea Creatures*, begin with a pair of stylized octopi (above). The 51-foot-long wooden balustrade is carved from magnolia wood and features a series of ocean scenes ranging from sea monsters to ships to mermaids. One of von Meyer's staircase panels includes a beautiful scene of a mythical mermaid and her curly-haired child (below); contact with floor-cleaning chemicals is starting to affect the lower third of the carving. (Above, photograph by Nicholas A. Veronico; below, photograph by Gina Morello.)

This fresco covers the stairwell's ceiling and surrounds a brass, Art Deco lighting fixture. The fresco contains the astrological zodiac signs encircled by an overflowing feast of delicacies, which would have been hard to come by during the Great Depression. (Photograph by Gina Morello.)

The stairwell and corridor to the restrooms contain a set of monochrome frescoes by Labaudt. This image of a beautiful woman in a two-piece swimsuit drying her hair at the beach was very risqué for the times; perhaps that is why she is hidden under the staircase. (Photograph by Nicholas A. Veronico.)

This fresco shows the faces of four beautiful and mysterious women who watch over guests from behind curtains. (Photograph by Nicholas A. Veronico.)

This photograph was taken on January 22, 1939—the opening day of the Aquatic Park Bathhouse. Architect William A. Mooser III designed the building, which is stylized to resemble the upper decks of a ship, in the late Art Deco style known as Streamline Moderne. The bathhouse is the centerpiece of San Francisco's Aquatic Park recreation complex; its $1.5 million cost was jointly financed by the city and the Works Progress Administration. Sargent Johnson carved the *Sea Form Marquee* frieze that frames the bathhouse's main entrance. (Photograph by Piggott.)

Three

AQUATIC PARK

The San Francisco Aquatic Park is situated at the foot of Polk Street on Black Point Cove. The Works Progress Administration (WPA) worked with the city of San Francisco to construct a recreation area in 1933 and 1934, building a breakwater/pier, bathhouse, boathouse, restrooms, stadium, speaker stands, and a sandy beach. The east side of the park is home to the San Francisco Maritime Museum's Hyde Street Pier, which hosts six historic ships.

Architect William A. Mooser III designed the Aquatic Park Bathhouse, located at 891 Beach Street, to look like the upper decks of a steamship. Visitors to the Streamline Moderne building are greeted by *Sea Form Marquee*, a low-relief marquee sculpture carved by artist Sargent C. Johnson (1888–1967) from green Vermont slate. Johnson was one of the few African American artists employed by the WPA art programs.

The interior decoration of the bathhouse was overseen by artist Hilaire Hiler (1898–1966), who was born Hiler Harzberg in St. Paul, Minnesota. The walls of the building's main level showcase Hiler's fanciful interpretation of the lost continent of Atlantis and the legend of the Pacific Ocean's continent Mu. According to Hiler, "the murals are neither primarily representational or symbolic, but decorative." Richard Ayer, Thomas Dowley, and Lawrence Holmberg assisted Hiler.

At the west end of the building, Hiler turned the ladies' lounge into what he called the "Prismatarium," with a color wheel covering the ceiling. A moving light fixture fitted with lenses of the additive primary colors (red, blue, and green) could be cast upon the color wheel to show the relationship of light and color.

Exiting the rear of the main floor lobby puts visitors one floor above Aquatic Park's promenade. The rear of the building is covered with Johnson's tile mural *Sea Forms*, and animal sculptures by artist Beniamino Bufano sit on the portico. Artist John Glut designed the building's interior and exterior lighting fixtures.

Between 2006 and 2009, the bathhouse murals were restored to their original, vibrant colors by Anne Rosenthal Fine Art Conservation of San Rafael, California. Today, the Aquatic Park Bathhouse displays exhibits from the San Francisco Maritime Museum and is open to the public.

The above image, taken on April 14, 1938, offers a look at the creation of Hilaire Hiler's undersea murals. Note the main entry doors and the three windows beyond them. Hiler continued the murals into the window alcoves and onto the sides of the staircases. Approximately one month later, Richard Ayer and assistant Shirley Staschen painted the background scene on the south-facing walls of the Aquatic Park Bathhouse. In the photograph below, Ayers stands and Staschen sits on a custom scaffold in front of a series of racks holding different colors of paint. Ayers is working on a sailfish, while Staschen is completing a series of tube worms. Note the mural detail in the window alcoves and that the construction supplies shown in the above image have been swapped out with paint and plans for the murals. (Both, courtesy San Francisco Maritime National Historic Park.)

This is a detail of the sailfish painted on the south wall mural in the bathhouse lobby. Note the spotting on the fish's upper surfaces as well as the architectural details of the now-submerged, fictional lost continents. (Photograph by Nicholas A. Veronico.)

Hilaire Hiler studied art in the United States and lived as an expatriate in Paris in the 1920s, where he cultivated friendships with such luminaries as Sinclair Lewis, Ernest Hemingway, and Henry Miller. He returned to the United States in 1934, and in 1936, he was commissioned by the WPA to direct the art projects at the Aquatic Park Bathhouse. In the early 1960s, Hiler returned to Paris, where he lived out the rest of his life. (Courtesy San Francisco Maritime National Historic Park.)

A building's staircase, walls, and archway form the background for this mural panel, as coral, shells, and sea grass decorate the painted passageway. Fish swim by as the octopus in the lower left corner sits at the bottom of the stairs in this June 1938 progress photograph of the mural. (Courtesy San Francisco Maritime National Historic Park.)

Details of Hilaire Hiler's fish on the south wall mural panel are shown in this image. French scholar Chloë Théault surmised that Hiler incorporated three types of fish into his mural: fish created by Hiler, fish created with different parts of existing fishes, and existing fishes reinterpreted by Hiler. Note the pattern details on the fish themselves. (Photograph by Nicholas A. Veronico.)

46

An overall view of the mural panel on the south wall, located next to the building's main entrance, shows Hiler's interpretation of plant life and how it would flow over the walls and stairs of buildings from the lost continents of Atlantis and Mu. (Photograph by Nicholas A. Veronico.)

Hilaire Hiler used a modified version of Thomas Gambier Parry's spirit fresco process to paint the bathhouse murals. The technique uses beeswax, turpentine, and varnish; enables the use of a wider range of pigments; and better withstands the harsh, damp, salt-air environment of the San Francisco Bay waterfront. This technique has been used extensively in England, specifically in the Houses of Parliament and at St. Leonard's Church in Worcestershire. Below, a stylized catfish skims the bottom of the sea, gliding past sea grass, coral, and a fallen log. (Above, courtesy San Francisco Maritime National Historic Park; below, photograph by Nicholas A. Veronico.)

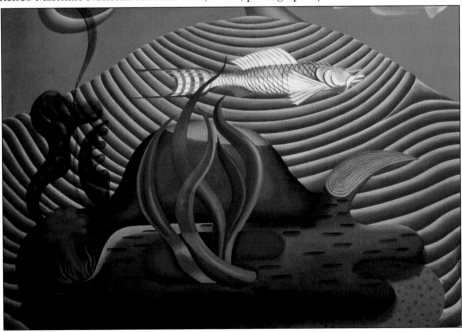

A Polynesian sea god floats near a giant squid in this section of the mural at the east end of the lobby. Note the rockfish and starfish at the bottom near the unoccupied conch shell. Hiler must have liked the texture of submerged logs, as he worked them into numerous panels. (Photograph by Nicholas A. Veronico.)

A crab crawls over a toppled column as a lionfish glides past a fan coral in this mural on the side of the northeast staircase in the main lobby. As a native to the Pacific Ocean, the beautiful but deadly lionfish could inhabit the lost continent of Mu. (Photograph by Nicholas A. Veronico.)

In this February 28, 1938, photograph, Moroccan tile mosaic artist Mohammed Zyani (center) and two unidentified assistants—working under the direction of artist Sargent C. Johnson—preassemble one of the murals using four-inch-by-four-inch tile squares. This work was done in what would later become offices on the building's first floor. Johnson called the tile mural *Sea Forms*; it was installed on the rear portico of the building and faces the bay. *Sea Forms* features sailboats, fish, turtles, and a variety of geometric patterns—all laid out in tile. (Courtesy San Francisco Maritime National Historic Park.)

This black granite frog sculpture faces a red granite seal, both designed and carved by San Francisco artist Beniamino Bufano. The City of San Francisco had leased this property to Leo and Kenneth Gordon, who were operating it as the "Aquatic Park Casino" as early as the park's opening day in January 1939. Bufano, along with other WPA artists, objected to the building's use as a private club, which led to a federal investigation that ended with the termination of the lease. (Photograph by Nicholas A. Veronico.)

Sargent C. Johnson's abstract fish fill one of the panels of the *Sea Forms* mural on the rear facade of the bathhouse. Guests enter the building at street level on Beach Street. The park's elevation recedes, so the building's rear elevation is one story above the water, making for tremendous views of Aquatic Park, the bay, and Alcatraz Island. (Photograph by Nicholas A. Veronico.)

The Art in Action display at the 1939 and 1940 Golden Gate International Exposition allowed guests to watch as Diego Rivera and his staff worked on scaffolds high above the audience to complete his massive fresco known as Pan American Unity. Rivera's membership in the Mexican Communist Party made him controversial in the United States, but his patrons, including San Francisco architect Timothy Pflueger, continued to steer commissions his way. The mural was destined for installation at the San Francisco Junior College's main campus at Ocean and Phelan Avenues. (Courtesy City College of San Francisco, Diego Rivera Collection.)

In the 1920s, Mexican artist Diego Rivera helped establish the Mexican muralist movement, in which the artists believed that public art was for the education and enrichment of the people. Many American artists traveled south of the border to study with Rivera or his assistants, bringing fresco techniques back to the United States. (Courtesy San Francisco Public Library.)

Four

DIEGO RIVERA'S PAN AMERICAN UNITY

In 1940, Mexican artist Diego Rivera (1886–1957) was invited to paint a mural for the Art in Action exhibit at the Golden Gate International Exposition on Treasure Island. Held during two separate events in 1939 and 1940, the expo celebrated the completion of the Oakland Bay (1936) and Golden Gate (1937) Bridges. Visitors could watch Rivera and his assistants firsthand as they created his 22-foot-tall, 74-foot-wide mural, entitled *Unión de la Expresión Artistica del Norte y Sur de este Continente* (The Marriage of the Artistic Expression of the North and of the South on this Continent) but commonly called "Pan American Unity."

The mural is a fresco mounted on 10 steel frames and arranged in five thematically continuous panels. It is Rivera's largest single-piece mural. The piece depicts the synthesis of the technology and industry of the United States and the artistic endeavors of the indigenous people of the Americas. The focal point of the mural is part machine (a stamping machine) and part goddess (the Aztec goddess Coatlique), representing the blending of the cultures.

The colorful mural encompasses a wide range of imagery. Interspersed in the mural are images of machinery, artists, dancers, laborers, inventors, spectators, and Mexican symbols and deities. An aerial view of San Francisco shows the Golden Gate Bridge, Treasure Island, Alcatraz, and the Oakland Bay Bridge. Famous figures such as Simon Bolívar, Miguel Hidalgo, Abraham Lincoln, Thomas Jefferson, Frida Kahlo, and Henry Ford are included throughout the piece, while the presence of Hitler, Stalin, and Mussolini alluded to the then-ongoing war in Europe. The mural includes Bay Area locals such as architect and art patron Timothy Pflueger and diving champion Helen Crienkovich. Rivera's socialist ideals are demonstrated in the mural by the depiction of both men and women—in different aspects of labor and of different ages, races, and occupations—working and playing side by side, showing unity.

The Golden Gate International Exposition ended in September 1940, and the mural was packed and crated in December 1940. It was to be installed in a library scheduled to be constructed at the San Francisco Junior College (now the City College of San Francisco), but World War II disrupted the building plans, which never came to fruition. Consequently, the mural remained in storage until 1961, when it was placed in its current home at the college's Diego Rivera Theatre.

When viewed from left to right, Rivera's mural breaks down into five panels. The top of the first panel begins with the mountains and volcanoes of Mexico and moves rightward from the south of Mexico to the US border. Moving down, the high priest Quetzalcóatl passes knowledge to tribal elders while Yaqui deer dancers perform to the right. In the center, Toltec Indians carve a human figure in stone while others work on a jaguar statue. At lower left, Nezahualcóyotl, inventor and king of Texcoco, examines glider models, while Mixtec Indians melt and mold gold into jewelry at right. (Courtesy City College of San Francisco, Diego Rivera Collection; © 2013 Banco de México Diego Rivera Frida Kahlo Museums Trust, Mexico, D.F./Artists Rights Society (ARS), New York.)

This image shows Diego Rivera and assistant Emmy Lou Packard at work early in the Pan American Unity mural's progress. Packard works on the gliders, while Rivera paints the cloak of Nezahualcóyotl. Comparing the full size of the mural panel on the previous page with the size of the glider's wings in comparison to Rivera and Packard gives scale to just one panel of this impressive fresco. (Courtesy City College of San Francisco, Diego Rivera Collection.)

Rivera's assistant Wayne Lammers sprays the plaster's surface with butenyl, which was used to keep the surface wet. Rivera would typically work for 18 hours at a time, and every effort was made to keep the plaster ready for his brushes. (Courtesy City College of San Francisco, Diego Rivera Collection.)

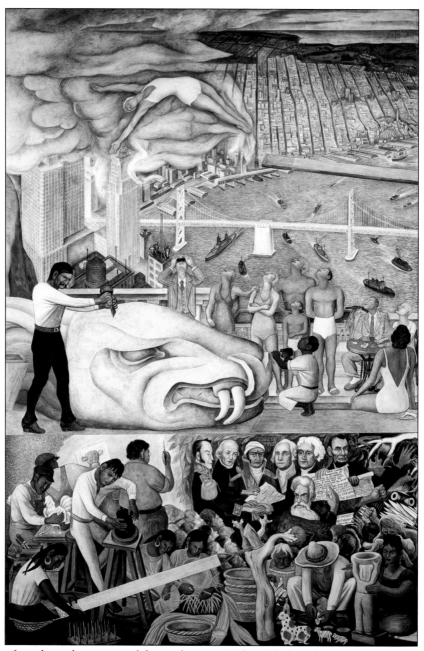

The top of panel two shows national diving champion Helen Crlenkovich in a graceful swan dive over the Bay Bridge, her body reflecting in the clouds. Under the clouds are two buildings designed by Diego Rivera's patron, Timothy Pflueger. The Aztec deity Quetzacóatl, the large serpent at the center, is being carved by Mexican artist Mardonio Magaña; the serpent's colored plumes flow back into the first panel. In the lower section, Rivera depicts himself as a painter working on a piece that includes North and South American patriots Simon Bolivar; Miguel Hidalgo y Costilla, the father of Mexican independence; George Washington; Thomas Jefferson; and Abraham Lincoln. (Courtesy City College of San Francisco, Diego Rivera Collection; © 2013 Banco de México Diego Rivera Frida Kahlo Museums Trust, Mexico, D.F./Artists Rights Society (ARS), New York.)

Diego Rivera poses with his sketch for panel 2B of the Pan American Unity mural. The head of Quetzacóatl is visible in the center of the drawing. From these drawings, the outline of the mural was transferred to the 22-foot-tall plaster wall to be prepared for painting. (Courtesy City College of San Francisco, Diego Rivera Collection.)

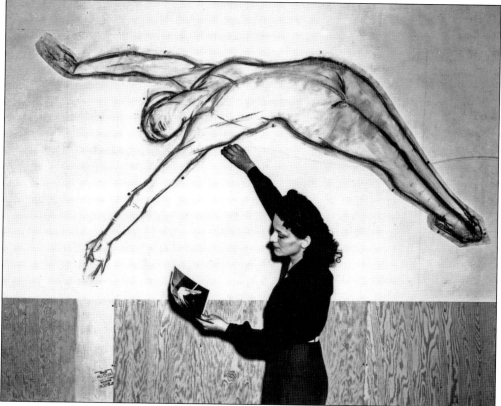

Irene De Bohus works on the large-scale drawing of diver Helen Crlenkovich that appears at the top of panel two. Rivera sent Crlenkovich and a photographer to the Fairmont Hotel pool, where the champion repeatedly dove while her form was captured on film; De Bohus is working from those images. (Courtesy City College of San Francisco, Diego Rivera Collection.)

The mural's center (third) panel highlights the Aztec goddess Coatlicue, who is combined with an automobile-plant stamping machine to show a face that is half human and half machine. Her right hand is shown with four jeweled calluses, symbolic of the necessity of working in soil. Dudley C. Carter, a fellow Art in Action artist, is using an axe to carve a bighorn ram, which later became the mascot of City College of San Francisco; the sculpture is now housed on campus. Artist Frida Kahlo, Rivera's wife, is shown in traditional Tehuantepec dress and stands in front of a second self-portrait of Rivera, who sits with Paulette Goddard, film star and wife of Charlie Chaplin, holding a ceiba tree—the Mayan "Tree of Life." Timothy Pflueger holds plans for the San Francisco Junior College (now City College of San Francisco) library, which was never built. (Courtesy City College of San Francisco, Diego Rivera Collection; © 2013 Banco de México Diego Rivera Frida Kahlo Museums Trust, Mexico, D.F./Artists Rights Society (ARS), New York.)

Diver Helen Crlenkovich reappears at the top of the fourth panel, arching over Treasure Island with Alcatraz and the Golden Gate Bridge in the background. At center right, Emmy Lou Packard, Rivera's main assistant, stands in a red sweater. Packard returned in 1962 to touch-up the fresco after it was hung in City College of San Francisco's Diego Rivera Theatre. Frank Lloyd Wright sits behind Packard. The lower third of the panel features scenes from two films of the period: Charlie Chaplin's *The Great Dictator* and *Confessions of a Nazi Spy*, which starred Edward G. Robinson. (Courtesy City College of San Francisco, Diego Rivera Collection, © 2013 Banco de México Diego Rivera Frida Kahlo Museums Trust, Mexico, D.F./Artists Rights Society (ARS), New York.)

Diego Rivera's assistant Emmy Lou Packard stands on scaffolding next to Rivera's portrait of her at the Golden Gate International Exposition on Treasure Island. In the mural, architect Frank Lloyd Wright is looking over Packard's shoulder. (Courtesy City College of San Francisco, Diego Rivera Collection.)

In this image, an assistant prepares the plaster for the last part of panel five. Rivera would later paint the remainder of the desk and the steamships of Robert Fulton in this location. In late 1940, at the conclusion of the Golden Gate International Exhibition and Art in Action, the Pan American Unity mural was crated and transported to San Francisco Junior College (now City College of San Francisco) to be installed in its forthcoming library. This library was never built, however, and the mural was stored in a shed until 1961, when it was installed in the school's new Diego Rivera Theatre. (Courtesy City College of San Francisco, Diego Rivera Collection.)

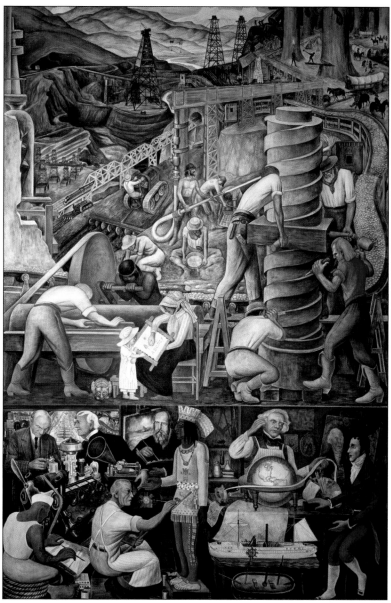

The mural's fifth and last panel captures the industrial activities taking place in the western United States during the Great Depression. The mechanization of the United States is depicted with images of the construction of the Shasta Dam, advances in mining (from panning to sluice box to hydraulic mining), the shift in cross-country travel from covered wagon to the railroad, agriculture, oil drilling, timber harvesting, and by artisans carving the screw for an industrial wine press. Below, the captains of industry—from left to right, Henry Ford, Thomas Edison, Samuel Morse, and Robert Fulton—are shown near the items that made them famous. Speaking of the entire fresco, Rivera said, "My mural will picture the fusion between the great past of the Latin American lands, as it is deeply rooted in the soil, and the highly mechanical developments of the United States." (Courtesy City College of San Francisco, Diego Rivera Collection; © 2013 Banco de México Diego Rivera Frida Kahlo Museums Trust, Mexico, D.F./Artists Rights Society (ARS), New York.)

Edith Hamlin is pictured at left on September 16, 1937, as she put the finishing touches on the second panel of the *Mission San Francisco de Asis* mural at San Francisco's Mission High School. This panel depicts friars educating the local Indian tribes. The activities shown in the murals took place one block from the school at the mission, more commonly referred to as Mission Dolores. Both panels were painted using egg tempera, with the first completed in November 1936. (Above, photograph by Brett Casadonte; left, courtesy San Francisco Public Library.)

Five

MISSION AND
GEORGE WASHINGTON
HIGH SCHOOLS

Located one block south of Mission San Francisco de Asis (Mission Dolores), Mission High School is home to a pair of 6-foot-tall by 24-foot-wide egg tempera murals. Artist Edith Hamlin, assisted by Jay Risling and Betty Willey, painted both murals in 1936 and 1937 in what was then the school's library. Both depict mission life, showing scenes that focus on agriculture, shellfish gathering, construction of the mission, blacksmithing, cooking, and educating by the padres. Hamlin retouched these vibrant murals in 1973. The murals were originally painted in the school's library, which is now being used for counseling offices; access to the public is now by prior appointment only.

Architect Timothy Pflueger designed the George Washington High School, which opened on August 23, 1936. Situated with a wonderful view of the Golden Gate Bridge, George Washington High School is home to a number of WPA art projects, including the Victor Arnautoff murals *Life of George Washington* (1,600 square feet), Lucien Labaudt's *Advancement of Learning through the Printing Press* (5.5 feet tall by 27 feet wide), Gordon Langdon's *Modern and Ancient Science* (4 feet tall by 10 feet wide), and Ralph Stackpole's *Contemporary Education* (5.5 feet tall by 27 feet wide). Dominating the athletic field is Sargent C. Johnson's 12-foot-tall by 185-foot-wide bas-relief sculpture, *Athletics*.

The symbolism in Arnautoff's *Life of George Washington* is historically accurate in its depiction of African Americans as slaves and Native Americans smoking a peace pipe with white explorers while other whites pass onto the frontier over the body of a murdered Native American. These images did not sit well with African American and Native American students, and in 1968, they demanded that the offensive murals be removed.

After the students took their case to the school board, a compromise was reached wherein the WPA murals would remain and "response murals," offering a different perspective, would be painted and hung in the adjacent hallway. In 1969, a number of artists were invited to present works, and from this meeting a muralist was selected. A committee consisting of students and school board members chose artist Dewey Crumpler, then 21 years old, to paint three murals that would represent the struggles of minorities. He began painting the murals— *Latin and Native American Panel*, *Asian Panel*, and *The Black Panel*— in November 1972 and finished in March 1974. Compromise saved the WPA murals, and through art, the spirits of many different peoples are now proudly represented in a school with a culturally diverse student population.

This full view of the education panel of Edith Hamlin's Mission High School mural shows the variety of crafts and skills the friars brought to the Indians, from blacksmithing, baking, saddle-making, and leather working to preparing yarn from animal fur. An Indian maiden is presenting a basket to one of the friars while others are learning to play musical instruments and copying manuscripts. (Photograph by Brett Casadonte.)

Hamlin's first mural panel depicted the construction of Mission San Francisco de Asis. Indian workers bring building materials to the site while others add grass for roofing and install the main entrance door. (Photograph by Brett Casadonte.)

Artist Victor Arnautoff applies paint to George Washington's coat in his depiction of the future president working as a surveyor early in his career. Arnautoff's *Life of George Washington* mural covers approximately 1,600 square feet of wall space at the high school named after Washington. (Courtesy San Francisco Public Library.)

The panels of Arnautoff's mural document Washington's life, from his days as a surveyor through his famous battles to life at his home, Mount Vernon; the mural also shows Washington giving orders as president. (Photograph by Nicholas A. Veronico.)

Artist George Harris assisted Victor Arnautoff with laying the plaster and preparing paints for the main panels of the *Life of George Washington* mural. The frescoes line the stairway of the school's main entrance. (Both photographs by Brett Casadonte.)

This image showing George Washington's life at home depicted many of the tasks required to run a plantation and the men and women who did the work. In 1968, at the height of the Civil Rights Movement, many students objected to black workers being shown in subservient roles (as slaves). Although the depictions were historically correct, they were not politically correct. Students took their complaints to the school board, and the two groups reached a compromise stating that Victor Arnautoff's historic murals would remain untouched while murals showing the struggles of other ethnic groups would be painted in the adjoining hallways. (Photograph by Brett Casadonte.)

While George Washington directs explorers into Indian Territory, Arnautoff shows white pioneers walking over the body of a murdered Native American while, simultaneously, a white man smokes a peace pipe with an Indian chief. New cities are visible on the horizon in this section of the mural that symbolizes the taking of land by force and predicts what would be done with the land. (Photograph by Brett Casadonte.)

Artist Gordon Langdon's *Modern and Ancient Science* mural covers the 4-foot-tall-by-10-foot-wide area over the entry to the George Washington High School library. Nobel Prize–winning physicist Robert A. Millikan, depicted on the left, is recognized for measuring the elementary electronic charge. The center panel reportedly portrays Academy Award–winning actress Claudette Colbert, a French-born American actress who was popular in the 1920s and 1930s. The mural has fared well for being nearly 80 years old; however, two stickers were applied to lower robe area of the figure representing ancient science, which also has suffered a deep scratch, and pipes block the view of the top of the fresco. (Photograph by Nicholas A. Veronico.)

Ralph Stackpole's *Contemporary Education* mural occupies one end of the Washington High School library. The fresco is 5.5 feet tall and 27 feet wide and depicts the base coursework in high schools: home economics, typing, electronic repairs, and other shop classes. Space for the clock was designed into the mural. (Photograph by Brett Casadonte.)

On the library's opposite wall is Lucien Labaudt's *Advancement of Learning Through the Printing Press* fresco. Labaudt, noted for his extensive work at the Beach Chalet, portrays figures from politics, science, medicine, and the history of the land that would become the United States to show the impact of the printed word on education. (Photograph by Brett Casadonte.)

Sargent C. Johnson's bas-relief frieze *Athletics* is 12 feet tall and 185 feet wide and dominates the south end of the school's athletic field. This commission was originally awarded to Beniamino Bufano, but the WPA removed him from the project because they thought he had incorporated a portrait of Harry Bridges, who had strong Communist beliefs. Bufano's student, Johnson, was given the commission, but not before his first design was rejected. This was the first major WPA project awarded to an African American. (Photograph by Nicholas A. Veronico.)

This detail shows the variety of sports played at a high school and amateur level, from boxing to fencing, pole vaulting, and archery. Note the dog between the pole-vaulter's legs, and when viewing the frieze in person, look for the cat near the tennis players. Johnson's use of cast stone enabled the sculptor to bring out detail, like muscle tone, in each of his subjects. Johnson also worked on tiled murals at the Aquatic Park Bathhouse. (Photograph by Nicholas A. Veronico.)

Sargent C. Johnson stands on scaffolding while working on the details of the hurdler's neck area in his studio at Fourteenth and Howard Streets. The 185-foot-wide frieze was reduced to 3-by-4-foot sections so that the heavy panels could be moved from the studio and installed at the school's athletic field. Note the Olympic rings between the female golfers and the relay racer. The east end of the frieze is framed by golf clubs and the west by oars from the crew racers. (Above, courtesy San Francisco Public Library; below, photograph by Nicholas A. Veronico.)

On May 14, 1948, Anton Refregier (holding banner) joined Congress of Industrial Organizations (CIO) longshoremen outside the Rincon Center Postal Annex to protest the partial covering of his mural depicting the 1934 dock strike in San Francisco. This four-day general strike is considered by many to be the seminal event that lead to the unionization of all West Coast ports in the United States. (Courtesy San Francisco Public Library.)

Six

RINCON CENTER

Rincon Center, a two-building complex that houses apartments, restaurants, and the typical storefronts that one would find in present-day San Francisco, is nestled between Mission, Howard, Spear, and Steuart Streets in downtown San Francisco. While its exterior shows the facade of a relatively modern city building, it belies one of the most controversial art projects of the Federal Art Project (FAP) era.

In 1941, the FAP held a competition to find an artist to paint a series of murals inside the US post office branch then known as Rincon Annex. The commission was awarded to Anton Refregier (1905–1979), a Russian immigrant and up-and-coming muralist from New York. This project, which would be the largest awarded under the FAP, took eight years to complete and cost $26,000.

The *History of San Francisco* is a series of 27 tempera murals across 29 panels. Tempera is a method of painting in which colored pigments are mixed with a water-soluble substance, typically egg yolk. This creates a thick, fast-drying medium that requires painters to work with speed and accuracy, as corrections are difficult.

The controversial murals are *Building the Railroad*, which depicts men of many cultures creating the transcontinental railroad; *Torchlight Procession*, which shows the triumph of labor unions in standardizing the eight-hour work day; *Beating the Chinese*, which, while it depicts a Chinese man being beaten, contains a painted note at the bottom denouncing racism; and *The Waterfront, 1934*, which captures the historic 1934 San Francisco dock strike and a day known as Bloody Thursday (July 5, 1934), when a fight broke out between workers and employers, resulting in the deaths of two longshoremen and several injured people.

Underscoring the controversy of these murals, the US House Committee on Public Works took up debate in 1953 to consider destroying the Refregier murals, as many felt they pushed a communist agenda and defamed the pioneers who settled California. Although the action was supported at the time by influential California representative Richard M. Nixon, but the legislation lost steam and was never passed.

Despite their controversial nature, the *History of San Francisco* murals were listed in the National Register of Historic Places in 1979 and became a San Francisco Designated Historical Landmark one year later.

Monks Building the Mission depicts the construction of Mission San Francisco de Asís. Established in 1776 under the direction of Franciscan monk Father Junipero Serra, Mission San Francisco takes its name from St. Francis of Assisi, the founder of the Franciscan order. The mission was more commonly known as Mission Dolores after the stream, Arroyo de los Dolores, that ran next to the mission. (Photograph by Brett Casadonte; mural subject used with permission of the US Postal Service. All rights reserved.)

Once Mission Dolores was complete, monks began converting Native American Indians to Christianity. *Preaching and Farming at Mission Dolores* depicts a monk speaking to natives as they farm fertile soil in San Francisco. Even this seemingly benign Refregier mural became embroiled in controversy when some Catholics protested the original depiction of the monk as too round and portly. Refregier agreed to repaint the monk and made him more slender. (Photograph by Brett Casadonte; mural subject used with permission of the US Postal Service. All rights reserved.)

Refregier's *Building the Railroad* portrays one of the greatest achievements of American engineering and ingenuity in the 19th century: the Transcontinental Railroad. In this mural, Refregier pays homage to the estimated 10,000 Chinese workers who labored tirelessly for low wages to help connect California to the rest of the United States. (Photograph by Brett Casadonte; mural subject used with permission of the US Postal Service. All rights reserved.)

Chinese immigrants had a strong work ethic and were willing to work for low wages, and these attributes kept them in demand among employers in the late 1800s. White people, opposing the competition, took matters into their own hands, beating and killing Chinese immigrants and destroying their businesses. Refregier's mural *Beating the Chinese* brutally captures these ugly incidents. Refregier included a quote from San Francisco labor leader Frank Roney at the bottom of this mural: "Attacks upon the Chinese I consider unreasonable and antagonistic to the principles of American Liberty." (Photograph by Brett Casadonte; mural subject used with permission of the US Postal Service. All rights reserved.)

Finding Gold at Sutter's Mill celebrates James W. Marshall's discovery of gold at Sutter's Mill, in Coloma, California, on January 24, 1848. As word spread, Northern California soon became flooded with '49ers, the name given to gold seekers traveling to the Sierra Nevada mountains looking to strike it rich. As the nearest port city, San Francisco became a fast-growing commercial hub almost overnight, welcoming clipper ships from all over the world filled with eager treasure hunters. (Photograph by Brett Casadonte; mural subject used with permission of the US Postal Service. All rights reserved.)

Refregier's *Miners Panning Gold* continues the story of California's past in its depiction of the most common gold mining technique at the time: panning. Gold panning is simple: A pan is used to scoop up gravel from a placer deposit, then gently agitated with water. Lighter material is washed away, while denser gold deposits sink to the bottom of the pan. (Photograph by Brett Casadonte; mural subject used with permission of the US Postal Service. All rights reserved.)

As a result of the Gold Rush, the population in San Francisco grew dramatically. With the influx of people came an increase in crime and corruption. To combat this, volunteers formed the San Francisco Committee of Vigilance, a vigilante group that took to the streets to enforce law and order. Refregier's mural portrays the 1856 killing of James King of William, a newspaper editor, by county supervisor James Casey. Casey was later convicted for the crime and hanged. (Photograph by Brett Casadonte; mural subject used with permission of the US Postal Service. All rights reserved.)

While California was far away from the fighting, it was still affected by the Civil War. In his mural *Riot Scene, Civil War Days*, Refregier displays the unrest in San Francisco between those aligned with pro-slavery leader Sen. William M. Gwin and those who followed pro-Union supporter Sen. David C. Broderick. With its large population of Northerners, California ultimately swayed toward the Union, particularly after Abraham Lincoln was elected president. (Photograph by Brett Casadonte; mural subject used with permission of the US Postal Service. All rights reserved.)

Torchlight Procession shows men picketing in support of the eight-hour work day. In 1867, the first statewide labor organization in California, the Mechanics' State Council, took to the streets, demonstrating against the Ten Hour League, a group of ship owners. Never one to shy away from controversy, Refregier included picket signs reading "8 hour day" in the original mural painting. These were later covered to satisfy authorities who felt the mural was too pro-labor. (Photograph by Brett Casadonte; mural subject used with permission of the US Postal Service. All rights reserved.)

At 5:12 a.m. on Wednesday, April 18, 1906, San Franciscans were jolted awake by a powerful earthquake. The magnitude 7.8 trembler caused catastrophic damage across the city, making buildings collapse and causing fires; the earthquake eventually led to the deaths of approximately 3,000 people. Refregier pays his respects to this tragic date in San Francisco history in the *Earthquake and Fire of 1906* mural. (Photograph by Brett Casadonte; mural subject used with permission of the US Postal Service. All rights reserved.)

It would take many years to rebuild San Francisco after the devastation of the 1906 fire. In the immediate aftermath, Army and National Guard troops, led by Gen. Fredrick Funston, worked with local authorities to support relief and rebuilding efforts. Refregier commemorates this with the mural *Reconstruction After the Fire*, depicting the temporary housing, food distribution, soup kitchens, and other aspects of rebuilding in the aftermath of a terrible tragedy. (Photograph by Brett Casadonte; mural subject used with permission of the US Postal Service. All rights reserved.)

In what may be Refregier's most controversial mural, *The Waterfront* immortalizes the labor movement in San Francisco in the mid-1930s. The mural is roughly divided into three sections: the left, which shows a man demanding bribes for longshoremen jobs; the center, which shows union organizer Harry Bridges rallying dockworkers; and the right, which memorializes the two dock workers who were killed when fights broke out on July 5, 1934, or "Bloody Thursday." (Photograph by Brett Casadonte; mural subject used with permission of the US Postal Service. All rights reserved.)

Thomas J. Mooney was a socialist, labor leader, and activist in the early 1900s in San Francisco. In 1916, he was accused and later convicted of the San Francisco Preparedness Day Bombing, which killed 10 people and wounded 40. In *The Mooney Case* mural, Refregier depicts the courtroom drama surrounding the 1917 trial, during which Mooney was ultimately convicted of murder. Many people believed he was innocent, and in 1918, Mooney's sentence was commuted from "death by hanging" to "life in prison" at the request of Pres. Woodrow Wilson. In January 1939, Mooney received a full pardon. (Photograph by Brett Casadonte; mural subject used with permission of the US Postal Service. All rights reserved.)

In *Hardships on the Immigrant Trail*, Refregier depicts one of the more well-known stories of westward migration in the United States. In 1846, a group of 87 people lead by George and Jacob Donner were trapped when heavy snow blocked their way through a pass in the Sierra Nevada mountains. Forced to spend the winter in the frigid mountains, 40 members of the party died in what is now known as Donner pass. (Photo by Brett Casadonte; mural subject used with permission of the US Postal Service. All rights reserved.)

The Golden Gate Bridge, completed in 1937, stands today as an iconic reminder of American engineering and ingenuity. Designed by chief engineer Joseph Strauss, the bridge stands 746 feet high and spans 4,200 feet from San Francisco to the Marin Headlands. In *Building the Golden Gate Bridge*, Refregier once again celebrates the contributions of labor, depicting workers constructing the bridge's suspension cables. (Photograph by Brett Casadonte; mural subject used with permission of the US Postal Service. All rights reserved.)

Refregier's *San Francisco as a Cultural Center* celebrates a number of notable San Franciscans who greatly contributed to culture in the United States as it shifted from the 19th century into the 20th. Those portrayed include, from left to right, actress Lotta Crabtree; writer Frank Norris; horticulturist Luther Burbank; writers Robert Louis Stevenson, Mark Twain, and Bret Harte; writer and publisher Hubert Bancroft; and writer Jack London. On the right, Refregier pays homage to the WPA and FAP with a ghost-like artist painting a mural. (Photograph by Brett Casadonte; mural subject used with permission of the US Postal Service. All rights reserved.)

The image above is a right-side detail of John A. MacQuarrie's 7-foot-wide-by-27-foot-tall *Stanford Mural*, which is located above the ticket counter in the Palo Alto train station. The mural also features Leland Stanford (below) looking on as people on manual modes of transportation (foot, horseback, and wagon) pass, eventually meeting up with the new mechanical marvel of travel, the railroad steam engine. Stanford University features prominently in the background. Anne Rosenthal restored this mural in 2005. (Photographs by Nicholas A. Veronico.)

Seven

Around the Bay

The Bay Area is unique in its concentration of murals and other types of Depression-era art. Diego Rivera's influence on artists of the region and the patronage of people like architect Timothy Pflueger resulted in a thriving community of artisans well versed in fresco techniques. Most of the frescoes were paid for by various federal government art programs and installed in public buildings, although there were a number of private mural commissions during the period as well. The privately commissioned murals are lesser known, not having garnered the publicity of the programs funded by the WPA, but they are just as spectacular and are worth seeking out.

Oil on canvas mural commissions enabled an artist to work in his or her own studio rather than on a job site, which was typically filled with construction workers and other obstacles. In addition, oil on canvas murals are less susceptible to earthquake damage and are easier to move, giving the property owner more flexibility should the building need to be expanded.

Of the numerous Depression-era murals throughout the Bay Area, many are publicly accessible, such as those in post offices and schools; however, others are more difficult to access. For example, the Presidio Chapel is typically only open to the public on Saturday mornings for less than one hour to enable couples looking for wedding venues to tour the facility. However, the chapel's mural—painted by Victor Arnautoff in 1935—is visible, during daylight hours, through the doors and windows on the east side of the chapel. Technically, this mural is publicly accessible; however, this example illustrates the need for visitors to call ahead to verify access and hours of operation.

This chapter also presents images of the murals painted by Dorothy Puccinelli and Helen Forbes for the Mother's House on the grounds of the San Francisco Zoo. These works of art are not accessible to the public due to seismic concerns with the building, but they are presented here as part of the historical record of Depression-era murals in the Bay Area.

In addition to the murals featured in this chapter, an appendix on page 94 contains a listing of nearly two dozen additional murals in the Bay Area.

The center of the Presidio Chapel fresco is dominated by an image of St. Francis of Assisi, or in Italian, San Francesco d'Assisi, who is best known as the patron saint of animals, the environment, and of San Francisco. A forest of trees and doves of peace surround St. Francis in this panel. Victor Arnautoff painted the base of the statue to read, "San Francisco in Whose Honor this Presidio, Dedicated September 17, 1776, was named." (Photograph by Nicholas A. Veronico.)

Arnautoff highlights the Ohlone Indians throughout the Presidio Chapel fresco. In this image, Maria de la Concepcion Marcela Arguello stands at far left with Nikolai Rezanov, to whom she was engaged. Her father, Presidio commander Don Jose Arguello, stands behind her. The original Presidio Army command building is behind the people at center. This fresco, titled *Peacetime Activities of the Army*, is approximately 13 feet tall by 34 feet wide and was completed in 42 days in 1935. (Photograph by Nicholas A. Veronico.)

The Ohlone tribe were peaceful native peoples of the Bay Area. They occupied the grounds of the Presidio and are shown in the mural weaving baskets, starting fires, and butchering a deer that was fallen with a bow and arrow. (Photograph by Nicholas A. Veronico.)

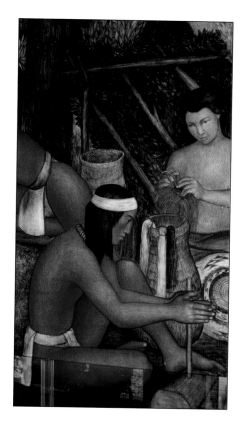

The right side of the Presidio Chapel fresco shows the then-modern Army at work. Engineers are showing an Army officer the design for the Golden Gate Bridge—note that the original design called for the removal of Fort Point. The bridge was completed in 1937 with a sturdy arch over Fort Point, saving the historic fort. This photograph shows only a small portion of the fresco, which also includes Crissy Field, the planning of the Panama Canal, and a soldier sending a message by radio. (Photograph by Nicholas A. Veronico.)

The Mother's House building at the San Francisco Zoo was donated to the City of San Francisco by park commission president Herbert Fleishhacker and his brother, Mortimer, in honor of their mother, Delia. Helen Forbes and Dorothy Puccinelli used egg tempera to paint *Noah and His Ark—the Waters Subsiding and Renewal*. The mural consists of four panels that illustrate scenes

This the interior of the Mother's House, a 1925 Italian Renaissance–style building on the grounds of the San Francisco Zoo. Over the years, this building served as a place for mothers and their children to rest, as the zoo's entrance and admissions pavilion, and as the gift shop. Mother's House is currently off-limits to the public due to seismic concerns. (Courtesy San Francisco Zoo Collection.)

from the biblical story of Noah's ark. On the west side is *Loading of the Animals*, which faces *The Ark's Passengers Disembark*—both panels are 9 feet tall and 60 feet wide. The south end of the building shows *Landing of the Ark*, while the north end features *Building the Ark* (pictured above)—both of these panels are 9 feet tall by 28 feet wide. (Photograph by Brett Casadonte.)

Helen Forbes (left) and Dorothy Puccinelli paint details on the right side of *Building the Ark* while standing on scaffolding at the north end of the Mother's House. The fresco was completed in 1938. (Courtesy San Francisco Public Library.)

The Science Building at the City College of San Francisco contains two frescoes—titled *Theory* and *Science*—that were painted by Frederick Olmsted as part of the WPA/FAP. Each fresco is 12 feet wide by 8 feet tall and both are located in the staircase at the hall's west entrance. Olmsted created them using tempera on plaster and completed the murals in 1941. This campus is also home to Diego Rivera's Pan American Unity mural. (Both photographs by Nicholas A. Veronico.)

In 1938, the University of California, San Francisco, commissioned Bernard Zakheim to develop and paint a series of frescoes on the school's Parnassus campus. His first two, *Superstition in Medicine* and *Rationality in Medicine*, were in Cole Hall. When Cole Hall was set to be demolished in 1967, the murals were relocated to the new Health Sciences West lecture halls. The frescoes were installed in two separate rooms, so guests can no longer view them together. This is his subsequent work at UCSF, the 10-panel *The History of Medicine in California*, which was installed in Toland Hall. (Photograph by Brett Casadonte.)

Bernard Zakheim (seated at center) and his assistants work on the concepts for *The History of Medicine in California*. Note the assistant standing at right and using a square to map out the front of the lecture hall in order to plan the murals around the steps at the front of the room. (Courtesy San Francisco Public Library.)

Zakheim's murals were considered too distracting to students sitting in the lecture hall and were covered with wallpaper in the late 1940s. They were uncovered a dozen years later, but in the process, nearly half of them were destroyed. Zakheim's son, Nathan, found the original sketches for the murals and restored them to their original appearance. (Photograph by Brett Casadonte.)

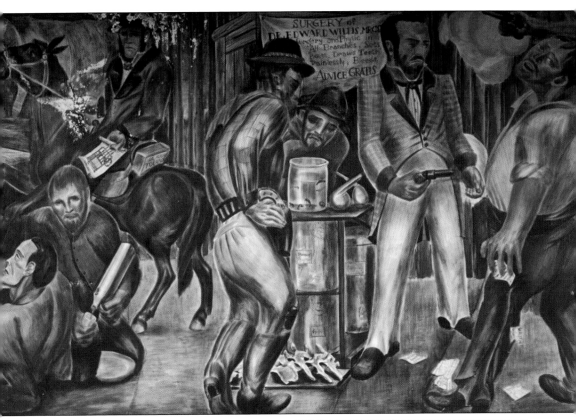

In the image at right, Zakheim works on one of the panels of *The History of Medicine in California*. This section depicts the quarrel between Dr. Edward Willis and self-proclaimed "Doc" Hullings at a mining camp known as Hangtown near Placerville, California. Hullings had no formal medical training—in contrast to Dr. Willis' extensive education and training—and he did not appreciate the new doctor moving in on his territory and clientele. Hullings challenged Willis and the doctor's friend Paul Clam to a duel. Clam went first, killing Hullings while being severely wounded himself. Dr. Willis' first job as the camp's new doctor was to save Clam and then pronounce Hullings dead. (Courtesy San Francisco Public Library.)

Jose Moya del Pino created the oil on canvas work titled *Flower Farming and Vegetable Raising* in 1937 under a Treasury Department commission. It is displayed at the Redwood City Post Office and is one in a series of Bay Area post office murals painted by Moya del Pino, whose work also includes the *San Francisco Bay, North* mural in Coit Tower. (Photograph by Brett Casadonte; mural subject used with permission of the US Postal Service. All rights reserved.)

The San Mateo Post Office is home to a Treasury Relief Art Project (TRAP) work titled *Life in Early California*, created in 1935 by Tom Laman. This three-panel mural was created using the egg tempera on plasterboard method. (Photograph by Nicholas A. Veronico; mural subject used with permission of the US Postal Service. All rights reserved.)

Oscar Galgiani painted *San Rafael Creek—1851*, a 4-foot-tall-by-15-foot-wide oil-on-paperboard mural, in 1937 under a commission from the Treasury Department. The mural is displayed at the San Rafael Post Office. Galgiani's other works included hundreds of landscapes and numerous portraits; many believe that his finest work consists of the two large murals he painted in the Stockton Courthouse in his hometown of Stockton, California. (Photograph by Brett Casadonte; mural subject used with permission of the US Postal Service. All rights reserved.)

Victor Arnautoff painted *South San Francisco, Past and Present*, oil on canvas, as part of the Treasury Relief Art Project (TRAP). The mural, which resides at the South San Francisco Post Office, is just one of many commissioned murals Arnautoff created in the 1930s. Arnautoff was responsible for such notable works as the *City Life* mural in Coit Tower, the *Peacetime Activities of the Army* mural at the Presidio Chapel, and the *Life of George Washington* murals at George Washington High School. (Photograph by Brett Casadonte; mural subject used with permission of the US Postal Service. All rights reserved.)

ADDITIONAL SELECTED MURALS

The following list of Bay Area murals may be available for public viewing, but some have restricted access. Please call ahead for access information and hours of operation.

Benicia	Dye, Clarkson: *The Legend of El Diablo*, Old State Capitol Building
Berkeley	Scheuer, Suzanne: *Incidents in California History*, Berkeley Main Post Office
	Rivera, Diego: *Still Life and Blossoming Almond Trees*, Stern Hall, University of California, Berkeley
Burlingame	Pawla, Frederick A.: unnamed, Burlingame High School
Hayward	Lewis, Tom E.: *Rural Landscape*, Hayward Post Office
Kentfield	Del Mue, Maurice: unnamed, College of Marin
Los Gatos	Spohn, Clay: *The Legend of New Almaden*, Los Gatos High School
Martinez	Hamlin, Edith: *The Road to El Dorado*, Martinez Post Office
Menlo Park	Albro, Maxine: unnamed, Allied Arts Guild
Mill Valley	Del Mue, Maurice: *The Golden Hills of Marin*, Tamalpais High School
Palo Alto	Arnautoff, Victor: unnamed, Roth Building (future site of the Palo Alto History Museum)
	MacQuarrie, John: unnamed, Palo Alto Train Station
Piedmont	Sheridan, Joseph: *Junipero Serra*, Piedmont High School
Richmond	Arnautoff, Victor: *Richmond—Industrial City*, Richmond Post Office
San Francisco	Piazzoni, Gottardo: *The Land* and *The Sea*, de Young Museum
	Wessels, Glenn: *Earth, Water, Air, Fire*, and *The Professions*, Laguna Honda Hospital
	Park, David: *Art, Civilization*, and *Nature*, John Muir Elementary School
	Poole, H. Nelson: *Harvest* and *Land*, Roosevelt Middle School
	Rivera, Diego: *The Making of a Fresco Showing the Building of a City*, San Francisco Art Institute
	Walker, George: *Education*, Roosevelt Middle School
San Jose	Garth, John: unnamed, Herbert Hoover Middle School
San Mateo	Herron, Ed: *Animals and Children*, Baywood Elementary School
South San Francisco	Littleboy, John: *North Beach, San Francisco*, South San Francisco Public Library